M000166407

How to be an Artist

**Learn to envision your personal
and artistic life goals, increase
your creative confidence and
identify the steps needed
to move yourself into a future
of your own making.**

by

Terri Balogh
©2014

Published by

Knowhere Media LLC
Denver, CO
knowheremedia.com

Disclaimer

This book is intended for entertainment purposes only. The author and publisher, Knowhere Media LLC, shall have neither liability nor responsibility to any person or entity with respect to any loss or damage caused, or alleged to have been caused, directly or indirectly, by the information contained in this book.

From One Artist To Another

Since I was as child I have created.

I have been lucky to hold onto enough of my own self through my life to continue to create and be involved in different artistic endeavors. Through those years I have been blessed with great mentors and known many talented individuals. I have observed my own experiences as well as the experiences of fellow artists around me.

By no means do I know everything about being an artist and I don't think I ever will, but I can tell you about what I have learned in hopes that you can benefit from those observations yourself.

Where You Are Right Now

So, you're interested in being an artist or at least want to tap into your creative side. The first thing you must consider is where you are at this moment.

Different people who read this will be at different stages of their artistic path. For some, the idea of becoming an artist may mean dramatically shifting their life and becoming someone that they, at this moment, do not fully believe they are capable of becoming. For others, it may be that they already identify with their artistic path but feel their focus and drive could use a bit of fine-tuning. Or maybe, you used to be an artist but somewhere along your life path you were sidetracked or turned away from your personal dream.

I wrote this book for anyone who has a desire to be an artist and pursue a creative life.

This is not a book about specific artistic techniques or methods. It is a book about the subtle challenges that many artists face, including myself, when they try to work towards their artistic goals. Subtle challenges that can actually completely side track and block even the most talented and highly skilled individuals from living the life they want to live.

In essence I wrote this to be a guide to help encourage others along their way, to let them know that challenges can be overcome, to inspire them to create, to give them a few basic life strategy tools and to remind myself to follow my own advice.

How to Start:
Stating What You Want

Years ago while I helped run a group studio/gallery I noticed an odd trend among some of the studio artists. The trend was one of self-doubt and creative self-denial. Later, when I took on teaching adult art classes I ran into the same situation. Basically, many people would hold themselves back creatively and I would hear these statements: "I don't have enough talent to consider myself an artist. " "I'm a fraud." "I'm not as talented as (put in name of some other student or artist). I don't deserve to be here."

These statements and feelings were big emotional hurdles for people to overcome and some individuals, despite having training and talent, never overcame this restrictive view. Many of these artists needed permission to be creative.

So before we continue on with this book any further I am going to give you what I call the artistic permission slip. Read it a couple of times, read it at least once out loud and then close your eyes and really take in what you have just said and how it makes you feel.

The Artist Permission Slip

"Today I, _____, give myself permission to find and follow my artistic path. I have a right to express myself creatively and to explore new methods, ideas and materials that I am drawn to.

I am a creative being and I have a right to my own creativity, to tap into my creative ideas and to express myself through my own personal artistic methods and vision.

By exploring my creativity and expressing that creativity through artistic outlets I naturally become an artist and I have a right to call myself one. I give myself permission to be comfortable at whatever artistic level I currently am without judging my work or myself.

Today I, _____, give myself permission to be an artist and to fully accept my personal creativity."

There, now that you have given yourself permission to tap into your creativity and to be an artist we can start exploring how to improve your artistic skills and how to navigate through your own personal creative ocean.

Establishing Your Vision

Why did you choose to read this book? What did you want to gain from reading it?

Something inspired you to start reading this particular book. Even if your honest answer is that someone else made you read it or you simply started looking at it because you were bored, you still chose to read this specific book entitled "How to Be An Artist". Why?

Some of you may have a clear idea as to why you started reading this. Some of you may want to be classical artists, oil paint brush or stone chisel in hand. Some of you may want to create art out of new technology, computer and hard drives in tow. Some of you may already have an established art background, but you feel like fine tuning your focus. Some of you may not want to try to make any kind of physical art whatsoever, but you want to tap into your own personal creative abilities.

The point is that whether you work with painting, ceramics, photography, digital media, film - whether you are a writer, a poet, a filmmaker, an actor, a musician, a fine artist, a graphic designer, or any combination thereof – whatever your medium and whatever reason you want to live creatively - it is possible to become an artist and/or a creative being who is true to yourself and who lives a creative life.

However, no matter what you want to be, what kind of art work you want to make, or what kind of personal circumstances you face, there is one common requirement that all of you will need to grasp. You must – absolutely must – have a vision.

Now some of you are going to say, "Of course I have vision, I want to paint a ten foot painting of a mule" or "My vision is to write a sci-fi novel about space pigs." Or "I want to apply my creativity to my back yard flower garden". All of those visions are great and I expect to hear those types of plans from artists, but that is not what I am asking you to envision.

What I want to emphasize here is that, no matter what type of creative path you want to take, no matter what kind of art work you want to make, you must have a vision, not for the artwork exactly, but for your life.

Your Personal Creative Life Vision Statement

It is time to write your personal creative vision statement for your life.

Take as long as you need to really think about this and include as much detail as possible. You can start by answering the following questions. If you want to expand your vision statement beyond these questions, I encourage you to do so.

First, close your eyes and think of your ideal life. What are you doing? Who is around you? Where do you live? What do you eat? What do you do when you get up in the morning? What do you do during the day? The evening?
Really try to see and feel what this ideal life would be like for you. If your mind is sending you negative or judgmental thoughts like "This is a fantasy... I can never do this." Then just sit for a bit more, breath until the negative thoughts subside and once they subside keep envisioning your ideal life.

After you have gotten a clear vision in your head, write down, with as much detail as you can, what your ideal life looks like, sounds like, smells like and feels like. Don't be afraid to write down even the craziest of details. Just let your creativity flow.

Please don't skip this step. It will be important later.

When you are done writing your personal vision statement, sit back, relax and read it out loud. Observe but don't judge any emotions that may come up while you are reading it. Remember, this is for you, let yourself really outwardly declare and hear the vision you have for your life. Later we will use this personal vision statement to build a more detailed life strategy, but for now you can simply let it exist.

A Smock Does Not
An Artist Make

Where I live there is a First Friday Gallery Event every month in the main Arts District of the city. I helped manage a gallery right in the center of the Arts District and I volunteered at another space down the street as well. First Friday in the Arts District was a fun event, and after years attending this event it became a perfectly good example of how some people just like to look like artists, but really don't do much more than that.

Many people think being an artist is "cool". I think being an artist is "cool" as well. Being an artist brings me joy. I love to create and see others create. I like being able to express my eccentric self.

However, a smock does not an artist make. Neither does a beret. The difference between being an artist or merely pretending to be one, is in the actual act of creating art. The outfit is optional and so is attending the art parties. Actually, the outfit usually is the result of making work.

You will find that the more work you make the more your overall look adjusts to the environment in which you have immersed yourself.

If you are a field photographer you will find that you have a definite need for that vest with multiple pockets. As a painter, the smock/apron/overalls will protect you from the inevitable paint splashes. When making a film that skully black hat will keep your head warm while you are trucking camera equipment across the street at 5 am to get the perfect sunrise shot and it's small enough to shove into your pocket when the day heats ups. That baseball cap you wear to keep your hair out of your face was given to you by an art supply shop. Of course it's covered in clay, you're a potter after all. Got it?

Dress however you like but don't mistake the costume for the actual act of making art, unless of course you are an actor or street performer, then the costume is part of making your art.

Facing the Blank Canvas

Do you remember when you learned things as a child? Did you have fear when you started out as a beginner when you were young? Most likely you did not.

When you are a child nobody expects you to be a master of anything and you don't really expect it of yourself. Mistakes are part of the learning process and you made plenty as you learned new skills when you were young. You may even remember learning new things as being fun and not really intimidating.

So what changed?

Through the years I have had the opportunity to teach art classes and workshops to both children and adults. I have taught everything from pottery painting to computer animation and design and I have noticed something, no matter what the medium, no matter what the subject, adults are harder to teach.

Adults have a lot of hang-ups and fear, and it is no wonder, as adults we are often expected to tell people all about how amazing we are so that we will get into the best school, get the job, get the date, etc. If we are in a career we are essentially supposed to be "experts" in our field, with the trophies, degrees, awards, test scores and portfolios to back up that claim. It is no wonder that when you have a group of adults trained to "be the image of success" and you reset the skill level to Kindergarten they freeze up and freak out.

However, even if you have strong artistic skills and knowledge you need to constantly hit that reset button and open yourself up to the possibility of chance, accident, failure and, ideally, pure curiosity and wonder.

This is the only way you are going to increase your skills, this is the only way you are going to find your own style and, when you get good at this, it can make life fascinating again.

Building Creative Confidence

Confidence, true confidence, comes from actually setting out and accomplishing something. Large or small, having any success at completing tasks that you attempt gives you a natural sense of self worth. Praise, awards and financial profit are icing on the cake, but they are really secondary to accomplishing a task that is meaningful to you.

There are two big things that can severely block you from successfully completing or even attempting creative endeavors. The first is a fear of failure and the second is an excessive dependence on the opinions of others.

Let us first address a fear of failure. Perhaps you sub-consciously believe that as long as you never try to do anything you will never fail. It's nice and comfortable to sit in a life of complete mediocrity, taking no risks and never stretching beyond your current beliefs, skills and comfort level. However, doing this is to live a life where you are guaranteed to never increase your confidence and you may, over time, actually find that living this way decreases any confidence and/or skills that you currently have.

In order to counter a fear of failure you must recognize failure in a more positive light. Failure is a badge of honor that signifies that you have attempted to accomplish something. It is proof that you stretched your abilities, took a risk and it can be a valuable learning tool.

One of my favorite artists and a powerful mentor in my past was once talking about pushing the sculpting material he was working with to the breaking point. He basically told me that if the sculpture did not look the way he wanted, he would just keep working the material until one of two things happened; either he manipulated it to the point where he was happy with the results, or the material would break and he would be left with nothing.

He then pointed out that if he stopped before he was happy with the results, he would have a mediocre sculpture and therefore have nothing worth showing anyway. His sculptures were amazing because he pushed the material he worked with to the limit and he never accepted a sculpture as being finished until it met his personal artistic standards. By working this way he not only accepted the possibility of failure he also became increasingly more skilled at working with and understanding his materials, their breaking points and how to manipulate them to achieve the results he desired.

Please realize that pushing your work and accepting failure as a part of learning is different than giving up and never finishing something. Failure is only permanent when you do not learn from it and if it keeps you from trying again, this time with the learned information.

Also note that pushing your work until you're happy with it is fluid by nature. As you gain skill you will naturally expect more from yourself and your work. What is difficult for you to achieve today may become a simple task for you a year from now. Your challenges will change. That is the beauty of pushing yourself and achieving artistic growth.

Now let's look at the other block that many face when trying to accomplish creative tasks; excessive dependence on the opinions of others.

Notice that I called it excessive dependence. This is because being able to take a reasonable amount of feedback, critique and advice will help you recognize the weak areas you need to work on and will keep you from becoming an egotistical fool.

On the other hand, excessive dependence on other people's opinions will make an artist lose sight of their own opinion and forever be doing backflips for critics (many of which may be giving out bad advice).

Remember, as an artist you have a vision, a vision that may be hard for other people to fully understand. So even though some of the critics may think they are helping you, it is you who must learn to recognize when their advice is going to help you achieve that vision and when it is not.

This might be hard at first because you may not have a track record of achieving goals to help back you up. If you keep creating, eventually, you will have a list of tasks that you have accomplished, even if they are small, and having those under your belt can help you face external criticism.

Hopefully you live a life where you are surrounded by helpful and encouraging people. Unfortunately, I am sure that may not be the case for some of you. If you are in a position where the people around you, and maybe your own internal critic, are constantly making you feel bad about yourself or your work then you may have to work harder to get over this block. The good news is that the very act of making work will most likely help you.

By recognizing these two potential blocks to your creative growth and how they may have manifested in your life you can learn to move beyond them. Doing so can be challenging, but it is possible and you are capable of it.

This brings us back to the idea of increasing your creative confidence by successfully achieving creative tasks. The key to doing this is to give yourself small and realistic goals that have meaning for you. For instance, if you have always wanted to be a writer but your family has always told you how stupid that dream is and you're worried that you will fail even if you try, then you are being blocked by both a fear of failure and external and internal critics.

The solution? You must write. That is the solution.

At an earlier stage in your artistic journey this may be easier said then done. When this is the case, you can help build confidence by giving yourself a small and unintimidating goal. Say... "I will write a short story that is 2000 words long or more." – that's it. That is the entire goal.

At this point don't even tempt your inner critic by saying that your short story must be amazing. Just write a short story that is 2000 words long or more. Then when you're finished, you have achieved that task with no pressure. You didn't have to worry about any other outcomes other than simply completing a short story.

After finishing that goal you give yourself another small and precise task. Perhaps now you give yourself the goal of, "I will now write 500 words that describes an interesting character in full detail." Keep doing this, giving yourself interesting achievable goals that challenge your current ability but are small enough to allow for success.

Focus on specific techniques or subjects and at this beginning stage, if it frightens you, don't worry about sharing your results. These small successes can be for you alone. Doing them often will exercise your creativity and help you feel more capable as time goes on. When you are ready you can move beyond creating for yourself and begin to share your work, but for now, you simply need to create and let yourself build an inner foundation of personal achievements.

Time is Your Most Valuable Asset...Treat it as Such

This is one of my personal favorites when it comes to deciding if or what I am going to do on any given day. When you recognize that time is valuable you will start to adjust your entire life.

Unfortunately, we live in a society that has convinced us to sell our precious hours too cheaply. We give up time to spend with our family, friends and to pursue our personal joys often for what is, in reality, a small monetary gain. I know sometimes we all have to work jobs and pay bills and, depending on our personal situations, we may work for less than what our time is truly worth. I have done this myself for many years when needed to, and I understand that sometimes it is necessary. I also understand how frustrating it can be for those with an artistic drive to spend their time pursuing other types of non art related work, especially for a low reward, monetary or otherwise.

In order to address that frustration you must begin, even in small steps, to find ways to free up your time for your own pursuits.

So, at this specific moment I want you to simply recognize that your time is valuable. I want you to work on adjusting your life situation as best as you can to help you spend that valuable time doing something that will benefit your happiness and the progression of your life. I'm assuming because you're reading this that making art makes you happy or at least is an important outlet for expression. Therefore it is one of the things that you truly should make time for.

If you are in the situation where you need to work two jobs for little pay to support yourself or your family, I still want you to recognize that your time is valuable. Make sure you take a moment, even ten minutes, every day to simply sketch, write a poem or brainstorm ideas on how you can get more for your time.

Ways you may receive more for your time could include asking for a raise from your current job, sketching while you ride a bus to your work, or actively looking for work that is more focused on your creative skills. Try to think of any way possible that you might free up some of your time for your own pursuits, pursuits that could lead to greater life happiness.

If you have extra time but you spend most of that time watching television, checking Facebook, or some other pursuits that are not art focused then you need to ask yourself, do you truly want to make art? If you do then why have you created distractions for yourself? Be honest and ask yourself some serious questions.

Get out a piece of paper or type the answers on your computer and really think about why you're avoiding making art.

Is this an act of habit? Do you avoid pursuing your art out of fear? Self abuse? Do you think it's a waste of time? Why? Or, do you simply want to think of yourself as an artist but don't actually want to put any effort into your art? If you want to pursue your art then schedule and set aside time and make sure you don't waste it.

At this point, you need to be honest with yourself. If your ego is attached to being an artist but you're actually quite happy being a truck driver then let the ego desire go and embrace your life as a truck driver. Trust me, if you can mentally tackle this concept you will be a much happier individual.

There is nothing wrong with being a truck driver. There is nothing wrong with being an artist. You could even be both but more than anything, no matter what the answers are to your questions, recognize that your time is important. You should be using as much of it as you can to live a good life that makes you a happy individual. What that means personally for each of you is going to vary widely.

Space is Your Second Most Valuable Asset

The importance of your studio as a physical and mental creative space.

Often when people think of an ideal artist studio they imagine a picturesque room dappled in sunlight from large windows. This is the classic painters studio but many of us do not start out with such luxurious dedicated space.

For a while my studio was half of a small kitchen table in a 12-foot camper. At another time my studio was in a cold, dark, damp and dreary basement below an art gallery. I shared this dungeon space with one other artist who was very talented but also seemed to be struggling with the tortured artist metaphor as well as a drug problem. But hey, the space was free and I got to show my work in the gallery, good trade off? At the time it worked for me.

While I do not encourage anyone to search out a dreary or confining space, you do need to find a space for yourself, a space that is yours, a space where you are free to be creative, to experiment and yes, even to relax into a creative state.

To start with it can be as small as the pages in your note or sketchbook, or even the digital art software on your laptop but at some point you will want it to graduate up to whatever you feel will benefit your creative mind the most.

You need to recognize this space should be comfortable, even sacred for you. What that means is different for everyone and also is based on what type of artist you are. Know that whatever space you choose to be your studio it is perfectly fine for you to go and be in the space without having the pressure to create. Often creativity comes from a certain relaxation, a sense of play or meditation, so a space that helps you find that state is truly inspiring.

Exercise 1:

Imagine your perfect studio and write down what it looks like, where it is, what tools you have in it, is it private or do you share it with others? Describe the ideal spot and how it makes you feel.

Exercise 2:

Keeping the ideal spot you wrote about above in mind, consider if there is anyplace you now have access to that could be transformed into such a space. Do you have any available space in your current home? Are their local places you might be able to rent? Coop groups that might share space that you could join?

If nothing comes to you that would work perfectly, or you're not ready to search or create an actual spot, then think about how you felt when you imagined the perfect studio.
Close your eyes and imagine you are in that perfect space. Observe how you feel.
Now think about places you can go and be that give you that same feeling. Do you feel a similar feeling when you relax in a certain coffee shop, go to

a certain museum, visit the botanical gardens, sit in a nearby park or listen to a certain type of music? Do you feel that way at a relative or friend's house, in a library, while riding the bus, at a rock concert? Write down all of the places that come to mind.

When you have written them down circle the places that you can actually go to on a regular basis and start going to them, notebook, sketchbook or laptop in hand. Go to those places and make a point of using them as your temporary creative mind space.

Learn From Your Mentors
But Don't Forget to
Find Your Own Voice

When you are first starting you will most likely be learning skills. Every artistic endeavor takes a certain level of craftsmanship to complete work. Even if you are essentially self-taught, finding occasional teachers and other artists to be inspired by and learn from can be very rewarding personally and artistically.

Your mentors can come in many different forms and at all artistic levels. Some of my best teachers have been humble little old southern ladies who liked painting on porcelain plates as well as highly acclaimed, world renowned sculptors backed by impressive degrees and awards. You may even find that your mentors are not exactly artists but individuals who challenge you to think and learn, to reflect and grow.

Having mentors and colleagues who you can talk to and who understand the challenges that a creative life can have are important when you need to talk about or have questions about your art and your life.

That being said I also want to point out that a great mentor will help you grow into your own artist. Personal insecurities may actually make an artist jump from one mentor to the next, from one university to the next, from one art form to the next, always acting as a student and never trying to really find their own style and voice.

While exploration and constant learning is good, make sure you try to find your own voice in the process. Any individual you find that can help you do that is worth their weight in gold.

Unfortunately, there are also mentor artists and teachers that may hold their students back, usually due to some ego insecurity of their own. Try to be aware of this and make sure you work with and surround yourself with individuals that encourage your growth and don't just ask you to be their clone.

In essence, find great mentors, learn from them, respect them, appreciate what they have given you but remember, at some point, you need to leave the mentor's nest. If one of your mentors tries to prevent that from happening then you need to not only leave, but stay away.

At some point, whether now or 20 years from now, or somewhere in between, you should be able to stand on your own artistic feet with your own style and your own artistic confidence. You don't have to do this immediately, but that is what you are capable of and that is what your aim should be.

Incorporating Your Creative Life into the Rest of Your Existence

You don't have to starve to be a "real artist", and nobody should expect you to, especially yourself.

Ahhh…the old "starving artist" image. Has this image kept you from embracing your creative self? If it hasn't kept you from pursuing your love for an art form, is it making you willing to embrace poverty?

Our society loves this tragic figure. So much so that artists embrace the romanticized image for themselves, letting it lock them in struggle and chaos and giving them the identity of being tortured beings who flounder around in tragic lives.

General society embraces this image as well and sometimes causes individuals to think that all art is overpriced or that you should do more for free than you can afford. You really can't blame people for having this perception, it has been pushed into all of our brains by "the starving artist" meme.

Let's think about this for a minute. For one, is it true? If it is, does it have to be? If you actually look at the lives of some of our most revered artist in history you will find that many of them had a savvy business side or at least learned one as time went on.

Don't be attached to the "starving artist" image, doing so will sink your ability to have monetary success. I also believe that this metaphor is sometimes used as an excuse by artists to ignore their own self-care and life responsibilities.

Good artists sometimes embrace this image and never take the steps necessary to learn the basics of financial wisdom that would help them continue in their career. Unfortunately, some of them just give up. Other artists use this image as a way to protect their egos instead of really looking at their skill level or new ways to present their work and themselves.

Are you being honest with yourself? Do you need to improve your skills, the quality of your work, the quantity, your presentation, your way of explaining the work to others, or your artistic business skills? Have you been focusing on one area of creating art at the expense of another?

For example, have you been making a lot of quality work but spending no time learning about ways to market or display that work? If you want to be the starving artist then by all means go for it, but don't be tricked by this metaphor into believing that the only way to be an artist is to flounder around in the mud (unless, of course, you work with mud).

If you happen to make art that is not what the world likes to term as "marketable" then consider what other ways you can support that art and yourself. Maybe the work itself is made of temporary materials. If that's the case you could photograph it or capture video of it disintegrating.

Look into other ways to share or teach your techniques. Give lectures, write a book about the creation process or ideas. Just, don't let your creativity stop at the making of art, take it with you into considering ways to support your artistically filled life. This includes paying attention to your finances and making sure you can eat and generally care for yourself.

Ultimately, caring for yourself and your financial needs leads to giving yourself the opportunity to make more art.

Remember,
Creativity is Valuable

The truth is creativity is valuable. Putting aside the "starving artist" image allows you to recognize this.

Entire communities and organizations are built on artistic endeavors. People look toward creative individuals for inspiration, not just to learn artistic skills, but to inspire them to live life, to see things differently, to find a new perspective. To walk a creative path takes courage, discipline, reflection and thought. Don't let yourself or your society make you think otherwise. Don't let the "starving artist" metaphor rob you of your ability to find personal abundance.

The Creative Day Job and
The Creative Career
vs.
The Creative Existence

In my opinion, even if you use your skills for a creative based hourly job, you also need to have an independent outlet.

The world we live in is based on some not so creative structures. Unfortunately, the very nature of many companies is not conducive to true creative thought. Even the "cool" companies that have pool tables in their lobby and allow their employees access to relaxation and fun so that their creativity can "thrive" often feel, to me at least, like weird hamster cages owned by people who actually "care" for their hamsters by offering them plenty of tunnels and wheels and little fake adventures.

I worked in one office situation that was very pleasant, lots of light and nice people. On one specific day of they week at a specific time they offered everyone free food.

After the initial "coolness" of this wore off it started to feel like I was working in a weird fishbowl, where all of us who hovered around our usual areas would suddenly respond to this "feeding", leaving our little areas of the large tank to gather and grab at the offered food.

Of course, there is nothing wrong with these company perks and they can help improve morale and creativity to an extent but ... and I am speaking from an introverted creative persons standpoint... the most valuable thing any job can offer me is to give my time back to me and let me spend that time pursuing my own independent creative endeavors and enjoying my life, my non-work colleagues, my friends and my family. This is where a lot of modern companies go wrong, because we are now in a society which loves being "busy" and many employers expect the attention and focus of the people working for them for much more than 40 hours a week.

So, then, what can you as an individual do to deal with this often creativity draining structure? Again, find independent outlets for your work and if your current employment is life or time draining... well, you need to start using your creative skills to figure out what you can do to change your situation. Changing the societal structure itself is too large a task, but changing your personal relationship to it is possible.

Trust me on this, if you are working at a creative job using all of your creative skills to create work, usually for uncreative people, and you never make work outside of that job, you will, over time, feel very unsatisfied with your life.

Be in Charge of the Creativity Spigot -
Breaking Mental Creative Slavery Bonds

We have already talked about the metaphor of the starving artist and addressed the value of creativity. Now I want to share with you some observations I have made based on my own experience and by working with and knowing many different artists.

First, most of the time the people who have talent do not know that what they have is uncommon. It takes time and experience working with other people in the world for an artist to suddenly realize that what they can do is a skill. If that artist is facing other issues, personal or psychological they may never truly realize their worth.

If the artist is also blessed with the ability to generate many creative ideas as well as the ability to express those ideas through artistic methods then they must and I MEAN MUST learn to value what I call the "creativity spigot" Why?

Well, at the risk of sounding cynical I also want to share with you another observation. The world will drain you dry if you let it. The people around you also value creativity, even when they don't know that they value it. Companies and individuals can profit from creative talent. It is why "cool" companies offer pool tables and "fun" stuff. Sooo....if you are creative and can create, the people in the world will want you to create for them and their agendas.

Unfortunately, uncreative or untalented

people will often see you do something and, because you are good at it, assume that you can do it all of the time, every day, under any type of pressure, for any reason. Your boss, your colleagues, your friends and even your family will want you to open up the creative spigot and let it pour non-stop. Not knowing any better, they will drain you dry, never giving you the important time or environment to refresh. This will happen, but only if you let it happen.

You must control the flow of your creativity, do not let it run out for everybody all of the time. Control the flow and what you focus your creativity and your talent on.

At best focus your creativity on your own creative endeavors or to support agendas you truly believe in. If you use your talents to work a job or take on other people's projects then do so in a controlled manner. Respect and value yourself, your talent, your time, your space and your creativity and only work with people that do the same.

CONTROL THE SPIGOT!

Otherwise you will find yourself burned out and drained, surrounded by a bunch of vampires who are pressuring you to keep creating and angry with you when you "can't perform". This coming from the very people who often don't know how you accomplish what you accomplish and cannot do what you do. Avoid the vampires and if you are already involved with some, find a way to take back and value yourself and your creativity.

Take care of your health, your financial well being, shut the phone off, change your job, make sure you get good sleep and if the world around you is draining you dry do what you can NOW to get back control over your creative self. Take control of the creative spigot because the world around you will always want you to keep it on full blast for them and their agendas. If you don't turn it down, or even off, those around you never will and you will end up tired with very little that you are proud of to show for it.

I have made the mistake of trying to "perform" for the world. The results were not pretty and I suffered for it, creatively and psychologically.

Now the good news.

When you take control of the spigot you can choose where this powerful creative energy is used, you can aim it at your own projects or you can use it to work on projects of your choosing.

Artists are creators and nothing is more powerful then being able to create something out of what appeared to be nothing. This is a talent you can take beyond the canvas, out of the gallery and beyond the film screen. You can actually apply it to your very life. Control the flow, aim your creative energy and create the life that will make you happy.

Agendas

Either embrace an agenda or disown it, but make sure whatever you follow is based on your own choice.

Some artists thrive while focusing on an agenda. Their artwork is inspired by politics, social movements, company and material goals, and awards or competition. If this is how you find inspiration and the agendas you are focusing on are truly yours (i.e. not being forced on you by social pressure or bullying individuals or organizations) then, by all means, embrace anything that brings you positive creative inspiration.

However, I would like to point out that some artists do not thrive in what is often the pressured environment that comes with everyday society and the drive to obtain trophies and degrees or work with material or political attachments.

For these individuals it becomes important to pull away from the pressure of general society. In order to stay balanced they must allow their creations the freedom to develop on their own, to burble out of their psyche or out of the very process of making the work.

This is a valid and powerful way to create and often leads to extremely unique work, expressions and techniques. To work this way means that you only work to create and it can be more difficult to do this than you may realize. You may become very self-aware of your own mind and all of the ways your psyche likes to distract you. If you have never attempted to create work this way then you should consider trying it at least once. You may find this way of focus very rewarding.

Getting Things Done: The Balance Between Perfectionism and Finishing

As an artist you most likely have a bit of perfectionism in you. You want to make work that has value and artistic merit. You want to make work that shows your skill, craft, time and effort and hopefully even has a dash of genius in it. You want to make something that matters and that matches your original vision, the vision that is driving you to try to create in the first place. That's great and it's a trait I think all artists should hold onto. However, that very focus on perfectionism can also be one of your greatest enemies when it come to another important step in your artistic growth, the step of finishing your work.

The reality is that for every masterpiece an artist has a pile of finished work that may not have been quite so amazing. We are often told about artists throughout history and then shown the masterpieces they left behind. Rarely are we shown the work that they pounded out when they were either 1) learning how to create or 2) just having an off day. However, you must realize that one thing all of those artists had in common was that they finished projects, maybe not all of them, but they finished a lot of them.

You will not reach any level of mastery without taking risks and when you take risks you will sometimes fail. You will not reach any level of mastery by not making work and in the very process of making work some projects will be better than others. Your vision of perfection requires that you hone your artistic skills and push your talent and you will not be able to do that without taking projects through all of the steps to completion, over and over again.

So, hold onto your vision but don't let perfectionism make you stall out in your tracks. "I don't want to finish it because it is not perfect" is an unrealistic, unproductive, egotistical and sabotaging mindset that will not make you a better artist and will only prevent you from learning the necessary lessons you need to learn to reach your vision. Plus, your very perfectionism may actually be blinding you to what is, in actuality, really good work. Sometimes the very pieces we think are failures are the pieces that turn out to be our greatest successes.

Finish the project, recognize the imperfections, learn from them and then start another project. Then, and only then, will you improve. Then, and only then, will you grow a body of work that people can view and recognize. Then, and only then, will you open yourself up to being an artist who has experienced personal and artistic growth.

Find Your Stomping Ground and Work It: The Artist and The Art World

Guess what? The whole world is the art world, and don't let any snobby art critic tell you otherwise.

At some point you may notice people referring to "The Art World", which usually implies a connection to a certain gallery scene, art focused universities, museums and certain Art Based publications. You may hear about people "breaking into the Art World" or "coming up into the Art World". All of this talk, especially to someone just starting out on their artistic path, can be intimidating. However, it does not have to be. Yes, some museums, galleries and universities may be hard for some artists to get their work shown in but not everyone needs to get into these places to be a successful artist.

Some people don't even want to get into these places and some people who do get in don't necessarily make the most amazing work or live the happiest creative lives.

What I am saying is that creativity and artistic creations can be valued in many different places of society and the world, not just certain galleries or museums. You don't need an art degree and you don't need an art critic's stamp of approval on your work (although, if it works out for you, having those two things are not necessarily a bad thing). I have known artists who were both financially and creatively fulfilled that never put their work in a gallery.

The point is that your creative energy and

your creations can have a place in the world, whether you sell paintings out of a city park, sell jewelry online, teach classes on bonsai trimming in garden nurseries, project digital art videos at dance club raves, or show in traditional museums and galleries. The challenge for you is to review your own art and try to decide where it will fit and where you would feel most successful showing, sharing and selling it (if selling is your goal).

Don't Fear the Gallery:
It's Only a White Room

Galleries are businesses that usually focus on promoting, displaying and selling a specific style or genre of artwork. If you have good work that fits their space they will want to talk to you. Research the gallery before you approach them and determine if you think your work fits what they show.

There are different opinions on how to approach galleries, some people believe you send them examples of your work along with a formal letter of interest. Other people will tell you to drop in during slow hours and talk to them in person. From my experience all of this depends on the specific gallery and the individuals who run them.

If you are unsure of how to apply to a specific gallery then I would suggest giving them a call and asking how they prefer to review an interested artists work. A short phone call can save you and the gallery a lot of time by making certain you provide them with the materials they want, when they want them. Remember, a gallery is a business and anything you can do to save them time or make their lives easier will be appreciated.

If, after doing your research, you are unsure if your style fits their space then go ahead and simply ask them. If you are polite, considerate and sincere but your work doesn't match their tastes they may 1) give you some pointers that you can take into consideration, or 2) let you know about other opportunities you may not have previously considered.

If they actually go to the effort of critiquing your work or your presentation and they let you know how you could improve, by all means, listen.

Having the insight of a gallery professional tell you what you can do to improve your work can be very helpful. Make sure you drop your ego and thank them for the feedback, even if their critique sounds harsh. Even if you decide later that for some reason you do not want to make the changes they suggested, you will do so based on a personal or artistic choice and not out of ignorance.

If you can't find a space to show your work, than make one. Yes, that's what I said, make one and promote your own work. At the last gallery I worked, we used to joke, "It's only a white room." While this was a joke, it does have a good bit of truth to it. In order to have a show you need a space to display in and a way to encourage people to come and see that work. It really can be that simple.

Search out spaces that you can use for however long you want to show your work. Arts districts, community centers, hotels, art schools, concert halls and many more community or art related locations often have spaces, rooms, hallways, lobbies, etc., that you can either rent or sometimes use for free.

Putting on your own show may take more work on your part but you can also have more control over the display and what work is shown. You will have to hang the show and promote it, create marketing materials and try to draw in a crowd. Think of this when you are choosing a space. Rooms in arts districts may have a higher chance of drawing in drop in customers who want to review art. However, some of you may find more success in non-art based spaces.

If for instance you create imagery that is inspired by molecular biology your work may find an interested audience at a location closer to hospitals, science museums, certain colleges and at science or medical trade shows and conventions. If you photograph rock musicians you may be better off seeing if you can have a show at music festivals, concert venues, music stores or in the parts of cities and towns that are known for having a strong music scene.

Coming to Peace with the Business Side of Art

Whether you are working within the gallery structure, showing and selling work online, or arranging your own live shows, if you take your art focus beyond hobby status you are going to have to come to peace with the business side of art.

Many artists will balk at the mention of also being business people. We want our artistic creations to be free of such monetary chains. That is fine... it really is, but you must be honest with yourself. How do you want to live? Can you live that way without making any or very little money? Does living that way support your creative ability and path?

Be completely honest with yourself. If you want to make art and never worry about making a living with it by all means do it, I give you my full blessing.

However, if making art your livelihood is what will make you happy then you must deal with it, to some extent, like a business.

The business side of being an artist is often a frustrating stage for many very creative people, but it doesn't have to be and much of the frustration comes from running into rejection or lack of direct sales. Remember, your goal is to live a happy and successful life for yourself as an artist and creative being. You must take into consideration how you will make a living. Making your living may not be based on direct sales of your art. That will depend on the type of art you make and the way you choose to display or live with it. Maybe your main income does not come from direct sales of your art, but it might come from a source that helps you free up your time and your space so that you can continue to pursue your art full time.

Consider the following – your creative work is an asset – think in terms of how you can make an income stream from that asset. If you are a painter then you most likely have considered selling a painting. That is one form of income. However, have you also considered making a book of your paintings? What about other items that include your imagery; T-shirts? Book Markers? Posters? Items that you can sell for a lot less than the original piece may bring you passive income long after you have created it. Doing this brings a second potential income stream from your painting besides simply selling the original.

If you make performance art you may consider investing in or creating photos or videos of your performance. Then you can sell that imagery or use it to promote your shows. Remember, your income from your art alone may not be your real bread and butter, but having income streams that come from your art such as lectures, teaching, presentations, books, post cards, online products, or replicas of the original can add up.

This is where you can use your creativity. This is where all of the work you've done to become an artist can come to your rescue. Allow your brain to shift your creativity into the act of making income and you don't convince yourself that you have to starve to be an artist, or worse, that you are a "sell out" if you find a decent way to survive. Plus, the more of this you do for yourself the more you will have to show to others, which, ultimately makes art agents and galleries confident that your work is something they may want to represent.

No matter what angle you approach your artistic business do yourself a favor and equip yourself with some basic small business skills. Make sure you address the big bad issues of marketing, taxes, business relationships, references, matching your work to an exhibition, gallery or demographic and ultimately, sales.

Be fluid, shift, if something isn't working, reflect. Changing your strategy, your views on art, the way you present yourself and your work may do wonders for how others receive you. Keep changing, growing, learning and searching if you want the best results possible and be open to streams of income from sources you didn't originally predict. They may surprise you.

Surviving Transition and Change

If you want to be an artist and you're not creating art then you need to ask yourself "Why?"

I have found that every goal I have ever made and attempted to work toward has required a certain amount of personal reflection, life changes and a bit of battling with my own personal demons. Even if I, at times, have failed at successfully achieving specific goals, the attempt to achieve them has stretched my psyche and made me question myself, my methods and, sometimes, my beliefs.

Artists, and their work, benefit from stretching their perspective. Many of us thrive on this activity and often search out opportunities to do so. However, even the most fluid of us have moments of stagnating fear or a period of time where our lack of confidence, life situation or just basic confusion on how to proceed has frozen us in our tracks.

The only solution to these moments is to be kind to yourself but keep moving, albeit slowly. These are the moments when you simply need to take pains to go through some basic motions or meet up with some artistic friends. Doing so may seem like a small step, but it will eventually help you move out of what can be a creative shutdown.

Unfortunately, these moments of fear and confusion are the times when you are also the most vulnerable to self-destruction. These are the moments of time I have seen talented individuals embrace unhealthy relationships with people and with substances. Instead of really letting this state of mind reveal a lesson or a chance for growth they run from the unknown and distract themselves with other dramas, anything to keep from focusing on internal matters.

What is positive about these moments of fear is that they actually are signaling to you an opportunity to gain more understanding and a better grasp on your own self. Moving through them intelligently will take you to another level both personally and artistically. If you can actually sit with these moments of fear and still make artwork, allowing yourself to be vulnerable and not judging your progress or subject matter, you may find that your work takes on a more unique expression. This is actually a great place to learn to express your personal sincerity.

*At some point you are going to have to be bold...
at some point you are going to have to walk through
the veil of your fear.*

You do not have to do this immediately, it will be less painful if you at least prepare yourself, but at some point you have to decide what type of life you want to live and start living it.

I have an analogy that has to do with jumping off of a cliff. There are more ways into the valley than simply jumping off a cliff. People who jump are for sure crazy. They may not survive and, if they do survive, they are most likely broken afterwards. While they have reached the destination, one could hardly call them wise.

So if you are not the type to whom jumping off a cliff comes naturally, that's o.k. You simply must realize that there are other ways into the valley. They will usually take longer and will require more planning and a whole lot of work, but you will most likely arrive at your destination intact, stronger and a lot wiser than those who simply leapt and were lucky to survive.

Then again, you might be a jumper, or feel so trapped that jumping is your only choice. Well, if that's the case, jumping might be for you. Just remember that it's not the only way to get to your destination.

Art Envy

If you're feeling jealous or bitter towards other artists you're not making enough work.

Ah the bitter artist. Nothing is as unattractive as an artist who can't take new artists with grace. I want you to say this next sentence out loud. "There is room for all artists in the art world." Now repeat it.

Common society loves to tell us how competitive the art world is, it falls right in line with the "you have to starve to be an artist" theme.

Naturally the art world is so competitive that you will need to starve and feel in constant fear of being replaced by the artist next to you. I bought into this until I helped manage the first gallery I was part of. Up until that point in my life I believed that there were not enough opportunities for artists that worked in the genre we focused on.

Then, as time went on, and the gallery offered different opportunities to artists who created work that we admired I saw an interesting pattern; many of the artists did not have much work and many of them completely flaked out when show time came around.

Yes, there is competition in the art world. Who cares? There is competition in every aspect of life.

If you're pursuing what you love you will find opportunities. If you can train yourself to be disciplined you will find some form of success. I have found that the areas which have the most artists in them also seem to foster the most creativity and are the most inspirational. Your neighbor artist/galleries success may help you find success as well.

Try this, the next time you feel bitter, angry or jealous over the achievements of another artist just go to your studio and crank out some work.

You may find that after doing this a few times you no longer feel this way. You may even forget all about the other artist or the reasons you felt all nasty to begin with. Honestly most artists who make a lot of work or work on large, time-consuming projects are too tired to focus on art world gossip or lost opportunities.

If there are some artists in your community that you do not get along with on a personal level then just avoid hanging around them. You are a creator, if you do not have direct opportunities then stop focusing on others and start focusing on using your creativity to make opportunities that match your goals. Spend your energy moving your life in the direction that you want it to be moved.

Keeping Yourself on Course

In another past life I spent some time living on a sailboat. My neurotic need to be involved in creating art had gained me a job teaching children's classes in a small town, but my own ability to create work was somewhat curtailed by my living quarters and a focus on an upcoming four month passage.

While on the passage I had many of my personal views of life challenged and my psyche was stretched, let's just say that not every day was smooth sailing. During a moment of personal mental breakdown the captain of the sailboat asked me, "What do you want to do with your life?" I answered, "I want to be an artist." His response? "So what are you doing on a boat?" It was a good question and one that I could not answer at the time.

You can, and naturally will, put your energy into some sort of endeavor. Simply by living you expend energy. Just make sure that what you are focusing your energy on is taking you where you want to go. My days living and traveling on a sailboat provided me with many skills that weren't directly art related. However, it did give me my metaphor of the creative ocean.

In the ocean there are no landmarks, there are shifts in weather, wind and currents, distractions of the occasional aquatic sea life and visiting birds. There is even the distraction of sheer boredom, the feeling that even though you have been moving you are not getting anywhere. There are doldrums of flat water and terrifying storms. There are dangerous rocks and the constant promise of distant lands. There are passing visitors in other boats, massive cargo barges, cruise ships, military war machines and an immense amount of space that you can float in forever. In essence, while the ocean is a beautiful and inspiring place it is also easy to get sidetracked or lost in its immense possibility.

For this reason, when an individual is sailing across an ocean it becomes necessary for them to constantly navigate and check their position in order for them to successfully get to their destination.

Doing so allows them to feel comforted when they have seen nothing but blue water for days and they are worried about their progress. Doing so allows them the ability to enjoy the occasional distraction without becoming completely lost. Doing so allows them to avoid the dangerous rocks and helps them reset their course if they are ever thrown off by an unpredictable storm. Setting their course and checking it often allows the distant lands they know exists to actually become a potential destination and not just a fantasy or a dream.

So what does all of this talk about sailing on an ocean have to do with being an artist? Well, the creative life is much like the vast ocean. It is intoxicatingly attractive, mysterious and inspiring and can take you to many different destinations. Destinations that you thought only existed in your dreams.

It can also be terrifying, overwhelming, and a place where it's easy to lose track of yourself and your goals. You need to develop and use tools to help you navigate the vast creative ocean. In essence where you aim your sites is where your life will go.

Wandering is fine. It is, as an artist, most likely part of your nature. For me wandering has allowed me to gather skills, experience, perspective, contacts and inspiration. However, occasionally looking around and seeing where you are and anticipating where you are going will help ensure that you don't wake up one day in a place that makes you completely unhappy.

As an artist I have explored many different careers that used my creative skills. Some of those paths were fun and fulfilling, some of them were damaging to my mental health and my creative soul. Those few required a time of recovery after I realized they were destroying me. What I learned from the creative death traps that almost engulfed me is that it is helpful and actually necessary to constantly check your course and focus on where you're aiming your life.

For example – you may be at a stage where you need to use your creative skills in an environment that is not quite your focus area. Most of us do this for a while in order to get our financial footing, to learn skills or even in the process of trying to figure out what our actual goal is.

Let's say you have been working on Graphic Design projects for employment and income but your real desire is to be a fine artist working with oil paint. I have had some artists tell me you can't do both, but I disagree.

Sometimes I believe you need to do both in order to take care of your life and to help transition to a different focus. Sometimes, the duality of the two focuses can help each other – working on pottery is often the first thing I feel like doing after I have been working for long hours on digital or video work. The two focuses are so different that one gives me a sense of relief after working for too long on the other. So in this way they complement each other, at least for me they do.

If you can control the spigot in regards to the graphic design job, or even better if it can help inform and inspire your other art, then you can dedicate hours into that field while you build up your skills/contacts/work that will allow you to transition into working on oil painting more often or completely. It is possible, but I will admit that working this way can sometimes be difficult and it can be a trap for some to get wrapped up and unfocused, lost in a creative success rabbit hole.

It is in these types of stages that it is vital to check your course frequently. Make sure you don't stop taking the steps that will aim you towards being a painter, make sure you value your private studio time and do not let the graphic design work seep into what you have declared your "painting studio time", or whatever the medium you choose as you ultimate artistic goal.

By checking in on yourself frequently you can make the small adjustments necessary for long-term benefits. The trickiest traps often lay in wait for you if you have gotten yourself close to your goal but not exactly. BEWARE OF THESE subtle differences in what you're currently doing and what you really want to do. If you ignore the subtle differences and get your mind just slightly off focus you could end up with years of time and experience invested in wedding photography when you're real goal and passion is to be a nature photographer.

Of course, being a bit off track is not the end of the world but slight adjustments to your focus could have put you in a different place.

So, if you need the money, have the opportunity and feel happy to shoot a wedding then do so, but if your goal is to be a nature photographer make sure you are actually taking the time to shoot nature photography. When you sign up for classes, seek out mentors, whenever you spend your valuable extra energy, money and time make sure it is with your nature photography goal in mind.

If you are working on and pursuing your art or your art career, if you are truly challenging yourself, at some point you will think, "What the hell have I gotten myself into?"

We were driving to the supermarket at 5:00 AM to buy food to support the actors and crew we had promised to meet at 8:00. It was early in the production of shooting our first feature film and the director and I had taken on multiple roles as independent filmmakers, one of which was the role of "Craft Services".

We were exhausted, but not because it was early morning, or the fact that we were a crew of two. We were tired because we felt miserable, our own personal psyches and internal critics had been attacking us regularly. We had barely slept and at this point of the process of filmmaking we found ourselves ranting, at least when we were alone together, "What in the hell are we doing?" "This is crazy!" "I hate movies."

In all honesty if we didn't have these great people waiting for us to show up that day ready to film the scene we had convinced them to do, we both probably would have given up the obvious nonsense of filmmaking.

Then, as time went on and we regularly ignored our internal demons, they finally gave up and went to bug some other not so determined creative mind. We found joy again, joy in getting the great shot, joy in working with a creative team, joy in being filmmakers, but, until then, the act was pure work, determined gut wrenching work on both a physical, mental, and emotional level.

So, what am I saying? Well, basically, this creative stuff, is not always easy and you will run into walls, exhaustion and the feeling like what you are doing is pointless.

I'm here to tell you, it's not pointless.

Keep going. Keep taking the next steps. If something has inspired you enough to actually get you to take the first steps then it is worth finishing. The very act of pushing yourself to finish will make you face your own personal demons. That alone makes it worth doing. Really, it does.

If your desire to make art makes you confront your own psyche and move beyond some of your perceived limitations then, even if you never make any more art ever again, that one piece of work has given you the gift of a lifetime, the gift of psychological health and recovery and self awareness.

What I am trying to warn you about and inspire you to overcome is the reality that creative work is just that "work". It is time consuming, mentally, and sometimes physically, challenging work. While some aspects of it will bring you the greatest joy you could imagine, there is a good chance that somewhere along the way you will deal with extreme frustration and pain in regards to your artistic path.

The larger or more profound the project, the less rewarding some of the steps may be, but let's put this in perspective yet again. If you "do" anything in life it will have a degree of difficulty, effort and discomfort.

Even a vacation requires work. You research the location, contact the hotels, book flights, try to budget money, arrange care for your house, pets and perhaps other family members, pack bags with appropriate supplies, get to the airport or other location at a set time and place, follow maps, get to the destination and fulfill your itinerary of desired attractions and/or explore unknown areas. You take pictures, collect memorabilia, send postcards, find your way successfully back to the unfamiliar airport with luggage and memorabilia in tow, head back to your home town, drive back home and then relay your vacation experience to all of your interested family and friends.

Hopefully, if the vacation was successful you achieved all of that and are more relaxed and happy then you were when you left. So, why do we like vacations if they are actually so full of "work"?

The idea is that you enjoyed it because it was something that you wanted to do, you enjoyed it because it was different than your everyday experience and maybe you enjoyed it because it gave you a new perspective on your life or changed you just slightly. This can even be true when the vacation feels like it didn't go the way you planned.

What I am trying to say is that you should not expect your art-focused life to be easy or to not require effort on your part. However, hopefully, you enjoy your focus so much that some of the work is either unnoticeable or at the very least the more painful efforts are countered with a worthwhile achievement. Being an artist may not be easy, but the path you carve in this world will be yours and that can make a big difference.

Holding onto Your Vision While Dealing with Your Current Reality

Congratulations! You have read the previous chapters and taken the time to both give yourself permission to be an artist and to establish a creative vision for your life. Now you're ready to move forward. Now it's time to dive in, address your personal current reality and start planning your next steps.

In writing this book I wanted to make sure that I provided some organizational tools that can help you build a life strategy. These type of planning exercises are fairly common in the business world but they are rare to see in art related classes or publications. This is unfortunate because artists can benefit and are perfectly capable of implementing effective life strategies for their work and their artistic career.

Now it's time to get down to the nitty-gritty, to really dive into identifying the actual steps you can take to help move you towards your creative life vision. The following strategic tools can help you plan your next steps. However, I do want to say that they take time and effort to fill out and require you to be brutally honest about where you want to go as well as where you are right now.

The good news is that you can come back to use these strategy tools at anytime. If, after reading about them, you feel like you are too overwhelmed then feel free to give yourself a break and come back to these tools when you're ready. You can also break out these exercises into pieces, working on one section at a time. Life changes take time and not everyone is ready to really work out an in-depth strategy for their personal and artistic growth.

If you decide to avoid creating these detailed strategies right now then at the very least make sure you give yourself just one simple goal that matches your creative vision for your life.

For Example:

"I will start a sketchbook and draw in it once a week." Or "I will sign up for guitar lessons." Or, "I will reflect on my creative life vision for awhile." Or, "I will start to search out places that inspire me."

Remember, You can ease yourself into the process of becoming the artist you want to be, the key is to at least do something. Take action. Every little step counts.

If you are ready to build an in-depth strategy now that will help move you towards your ultimate vision then continue on to these next exercises.

First:

Review the creative life vision that I asked you to write out in the beginning of the book. See if anything has changed for you that would make you want to adjust that vision. It's okay to adjust this vision from time to time as you learn more about your creative self and your art. After you have adjusted it, if needed, sit with the vision for a bit until it is clear in your mind again. Then you can continue.

Now that you have your vision clear in your

head don't worry if it seems too far or out of reach. Realize that getting to any destination, no matter how distant it seems, will require you to take a series of smaller steps. If your creative life vision is completely different than the life you are currently living then you will have more steps to take in order to adjust your life over time. The trick that you face now is in identifying the specific steps to take.

Identifying Your
Long-Term Goals

You can identify your next steps by breaking down your creative life vision into a few manageable long-term goals (usually more than three years away). These long-term goals should address key important points included in your vision statement.

Don't worry if you do not address all of the key points at once. Picking just a few to start will be effective and you can always return to the exercise to address more details later.

To do this start with identifying a few long-term goals that would support a piece of your creative life vision. Then describe your current situation directly related to the identified goal.

Example:

John's creative life vision mainly focused on writing, recording and selling his own music, having a happy and fulfilling family life, being regularly inspired by nature and being financially sound. (Hopefully his description was more detailed but for simplicity sake we will only pull out those general key points)

Now John can take those key points and identify them as long-term goals. He also needs to identify where he currently is in regards to achieving those goals.

John's Long-Term Goal # 1 – To be successfully writing, recording and selling his own music.

Currently – John writes music and has skill playing the guitar and singing. He does not regularly record his work and only plays live in small coffee shops from time to time (usually for tips).

Long-Term Goal # 2 – To have a happy and fulfilling family life.

Currently – John is happily married and has a two-year old daughter. He want's to continue having a happy home life but worries that focusing on his dream of being a musician will interfere and disrupt family time.

Long-Term Goal # 3 – To be regularly inspired by nature.

Currently – John and his family live in a small apartment in a busy city. He finds the atmosphere stressful and uninspiring. He finds that he is invigorated by nature and wants to find a way to spend more time in natural environments.

Long-Term Goal # 4 – To be financially sound.

Currently – John and his wife both have jobs but they also have a lot of debt. John works in construction but would rather make his living as a musician. This is an area of stress and guilt for him and his worries about money often block his ability to create.

Note: It is very important to be honest with yourself when you are describing your current situation. If your current situation includes negative feelings or sabotaging self talk then make sure you address them. Being honest about where you are is necessary to help yourself find the vital first steps that can help you.

Identifying Your
Short-Term Goals

After a few long-term goals are identified you can break them down even further into short-term goals (Two Year, One Year, Six months, Three months, One month and then, finally, what you are going to do in the next three weeks).

Working backwards in time will help you keep hold of your original vision while getting a better grasp on what you can do today to move yourself towards that vision.

This may seem complicated at first but if you do it correctly it can give you a handy checklist of steps. Ultimately, this is a tool that can keep you focused and allow you to occasionally adjust yourself from time to time as needed.

Keeping your current reality in mind fill in the gaps with short-term goals that will start moving you towards reaching the long-term goals that you identified.

Example:

John's Long-Term Goal # 1 (3 to 5 years)– To be successfully writing, recording and selling his own music.

3 years – In 3 years John wants to have a full album of original work ready to sell online as well as some CD's for promotion and for sale when he sings live.

2 years – In 2 years John wants to be recording his first album. By this time he wants to have increased his contacts with recording studios and/or his knowledge of the recording and album making process.

1 year – In 1 year John wants to have 10 to 12 original songs written for a full album. He wants to better understand the recording process and what he needs to do to create his first album.

6 months – In 6 months John wants to have 6 songs written (he plans on writing one a month for the rest of the year) and to have reached out to at least one recording studio/sound engineer to learn more about the process and/or read a book or signed up for a workshop teaching music recording.

3 months - In 3 month John wants to have 3 songs written. (he plans on writing one a month for the rest of the year) He will also continue to research recording studios and learning opportunities.

1 month – In 1 month John wants to have One new song written

In the next 3 weeks – John is going to work on writing a new song at least a couple of hours every week. He is going to also look for decent resources that can help him learn more about recording music – books, classes, workshops or personal mentors.

Currently – John writes music and has skill playing the guitar and singing. He does not regularly record his work and only plays live in small coffee shops from time to time (usually for tips).

Long-Term Goal # 2 – To have a happy and fulfilling family life.

3 years - In 3 years John, if all of his other plans are on track, should have his full album recorded and they may be already moved or getting close to moving to a new place.

At this point he anticipates a lot of change could possibly occur to their lives. He would like to make sure to spend some real quality time with his family adjusting to their new home. If he does have the album recorded he would like to also celebrate that accomplishment with them.

2 years - In 2 years (if it is decided that they can and want to move) John wants to have conducted research on the locations they are considering and how those places best match their work and family goals. Are there good schools, access to fun places for his daughter to play, is the new location convenient for his wife in regards to her needs and work situation, etc.

Again, he wants to share and celebrate any music success with his family.

1 year - In 1 year John wants to make sure that his plans for moving (listed under his goals for being inspired by nature) are in line with the welfare of his family.

He wants to talk to his wife about their financial and work related needs. He wants to celebrate any success he has had with his music with a fun family outing.

6 months - In 6 months John wants to share his newly written songs with his wife and daughter.

3 months – In 3 months John wants to make sure that any concerns his wife may have are being addressed and that they will continue to have positive open communication about any changes that are happening. He wants to make sure that she is aware of his desire to move in the future and make sure she is a part of the process in deciding where and when they might move.

1 month - In 1 month John wants to continue to keep communication open with his wife about his plans. He would also like to successfully share his passion for music with his wife and daughter.

In the next 3 weeks – In the next three weeks John wants to talk with his wife about his ideas and plans to reach his creative vision. He wants to ask her how she feels about it and if she has any reservations or concerns. He wants to know what those concerns are and see if they can find some solutions to any potential problems.

Currently – John is happily married and has a two-year old daughter. He wants to continue having a happy home life but worries that focusing on his dream of being a musician will interfere and disrupt family time.

Long-Term Goal # 3 – To be regularly inspired by nature.

3 years – In 3 years John would like to have moved, or be about to move, to a location that allows him to be closer to nature. (An apartment/house with a garden/patio/yard or deck, or a location that is closer to parks, nature preserves or other locations he loves).

2 years - In 2 years John wants to have identified possible locations that he and his family would like to move to. He would like to start narrowing down choices with his wife and take the needed steps to prepare himself and his family. If the desired location is farther from his work than he would like then he will consider looking for new employment.

1 year - In 1 year John wants to determine if moving to a more inspiring location is possible for him and his family. He wants to review what it would cost to move and start working on saving money for the transition.

6 months – In 6 months he would like to have been able to adjust his life so that he can now spend a few hours every other week in an inspiring location. He will continue to look for new places that help inspire his music.

3 months – In 3 months he wants to make it a regular habit to spend at least a few hours every month in one of the inspiring locations he has found both by himself and with his family. He would like to talk to his wife about moving in the future to a place that allows them to experience nature more often.

1 month - In 1 month he would like to take his family to one of the inspiring places he has found. (the zoo, the botanical gardens, a nice park or a drive out of town)

In the next 3 weeks - John wants to find places around where he lives that help him reconnect with and be inspired by nature. He would like to find places that he can occasionally visit on his own as well as with his wife and daughter.

Currently – John and his family live in a small, dark apartment in a busy city. He finds the atmosphere stressful and uninspiring.

Long-Term Goal # 4 – To be financially sound.

3 years – In 3 years John wants to have at least one of their larger debts paid off. He would also like to be researching and learning about different ways to sell his music both online and at live events.

2 years – In 2 years John wants to think of ways to increase his income. He may consider asking for a raise, pursuing a new job that pays more or searching for and taking on more music related gigs that pay. He would like to continue to pay down his debts and adjust his financial plan as needed.

1 year - In 1 year John would like to review his finances again and determine if any changes to their financial plan is needed. He would like to determine how much he would need to put towards their debts in order to pay of at least one of them off in the next two years.

He also wants to have a clearer idea on how much money he may need for a potential move in the future as well as a better understanding of the costs he may have in regards to recording his album.

6 months – In 6 months John would like to start implementing a financial plan that helps them lower their debts and he wants to start building an emergency savings account.

3 months – John wants to start considering ways they can reduce their debt and make the most out of their incomes. At this point he may consider finding and talking to a financial advisor or doing some research of managing personal finances on his own. He wants to make sure that they are no longer taking on new debt. He also wants to review their spending to make sure that they are living within their means.

1 month - In one month John wants to start saving any of the money he makes from his coffee shop guitar gigs for future music recording and promoting needs. He may consider opening a checking or savings account specifically for this money.

In the next 3 weeks - John wants to review his finances and see exactly where he and his family stand in regards to their income, their debts and their savings.

Currently – John and his wife both have jobs but they also have a lot of debt. John works in construction but would rather make his living as a musician. This is an area of stress and guilt for him and often blocks his ability to create.

Hopefully by reviewing the provided examples you can see how John's overall vision could be split into different goals and that those goals could then be broken down into smaller steps that he could take over time.

By doing these life strategy exercises for yourself you can start finding ways to work towards your artistic and creative existence right away. You can also use this same break down method towards achieving large artistic projects.

Of course, life does not always follow even the best laid plans. Things happen that may drastically change John's ability to act upon and achieve all of his listed goals. He could lose his job and need to reconsider some of his financial plans. He may find that after spending a year going to inspiring locations he has found a way to inspire his art without needing to move and therefore does not need to leave his current apartment.

He may find that he is overwhelmed with making too many changes at once and therefore needs to only focus on one key point for the first six months.

Or maybe, (and this is a very common occurrence) taking these first steps to implement change in his life has brought him to some opportunities that are helping him achieve his life vision in ways he couldn't even consider before.

The point is that going through these exercises is not supposed to lock you into an inadaptable mindset. Instead, building these strategies is a way for you to readjust your focus on your life and make sure that the choices you are making are in line with your creative life vision. Completing these exercises helps you break a big vision into bite sized and manageable pieces, some of which you should be able to act on immediately.

Your Personal Worksheets

Now it is your turn. Fill out the first worksheet with your creative life visions key points, a few long-term goals that address those key points and a description of your current situation in regards to those goals.

After the first worksheet is filled out then use the second worksheet to identify your short-term goals. Working backwards, break down the long-term goals into reasonable shorter-term goals. These short-term steps should be broken down into time frames of 2 Year, 1 Year, 6 months, 3 months, 1 month and then, finally, what are you going to do in the next 3 weeks.

Identifying Your Long-Term Goals

Identify some long-term goals (over 3 years from now) that address some key points or themes that are prominent in your creative life vision statement:

1:

2:

3:

4:

Now, match those long-term goals with a description
of your current reality:

Long-Term Goal # 1 –

Currently –

Long-Term Goal # 2 –

Currently –

Long-Term Goal # 3 –

Currently –

Long-Term Goal # 4 –

Currently –

Note: It is very important to be honest with yourself when you are describing your current situation. If your current situation includes negative feelings or sabotaging self talk then make sure you address them. Being honest about where you are is necessary to help yourself find the vital first steps that can help you.

Identifying Your
Short-Term Goals

Starting with one of your long-term goals work backwards in time while keeping your current reality in mind. Fill in the gaps to identify some short-term goals you can achieve over time (2 years, 1 year, 6 months, 3 months, 1 month and then, finally, what are you going to do in the next three weeks)

Once you've completed short-term goals for one of your long-term goals, you'll have a good outline to guide you on how to create a list like this for each of your current long-term goals and any you develop in the future.

Long-Term Goal (3 to 5 years)–

3 years –

2 year –

1 year –

6 months –

3 months –

1 month –

In the next 3 weeks –

Currently –

Note: Keep in mind your other life obligations and make sure that you give yourself a reasonable amount of time to achieve your short-term goals. Making sure that the short-term goals are achievable will help you stay motivated, keep you from quitting and therefore will be more affective over time.

In Conclusion

You made it. Wow!

You have read this book and, if you followed the above advice, you have made some form of plan to start, continue or re-adjust your journey as an artist.

Remember, even the most simple and humble of steps can make a big difference in your life and by valuing yourself, your art and your creative nature you naturally encourage others to do so as well.

At this time I actually want to say "Thank You!" I'm honored that you gave this book a chance to help you find and follow your own artistic path. As an artist who has been blessed with the insight and guidance of many great mentors, I feel it is important to give back by encouraging and inspiring other artists around me.

For that reason I hope that you found at least a few valuable insights and/or tools in this book. All I ask is that if one little thing I have said has inspired you to live a more fulfilled life then someday please pass that inspiration or knowledge on to someone else who may be trying to find their creative footing.

Good luck and here's to wishing you a fulfilling, inspiring and creative future!

The End

For more books and films by Terri Balogh, or for additional information, please visit knowheremedia.com

24296724R00059

Made in the USA
San Bernardino, CA
20 September 2015